follow me

Our World

CAROLINE GRIMSHAW

World Book

in association with

W C N

follow me and find out (almost) everything about your world!

follow me

Our World

CREATIVE AND EDITORIAL DIRECTOR
CONCEPT/FORMAT/DESIGN/TEXT
CAROLINE GRIMSHAW

SCIENCE CONSULTANT
JOHN STRINGER UNIVERSITY OF WARWICK, U.K.

TEXT EDITORS
IQBAL HUSSAIN AND **ROBERT SVED**

ILLUSTRATIONS
NICK DUFFY ◊ SPIKE GERRELL
CAROLINE GRIMSHAW

THANKS TO
LAURA CARTWRIGHT PICTURE RESEARCH
BRONWEN LEWIS EDITORIAL SUPPORT
PATRICIA OHLENROTH WORLD BOOK, INC.

TITLES IN THIS SERIES
◊ YOU AND ME
◊ OUR WORLD

FIRST PUBLISHED IN THE UNITED STATES AND CANADA BY
WORLD BOOK, INC.
525 W. MONROE
CHICAGO, IL 60661
IN ASSOCIATION WITH TWO-CAN PUBLISHING LTD.

COPYRIGHT © CAROLINE GRIMSHAW 1997

FOR INFORMATION ON OTHER WORLD BOOK PRODUCTS,
CALL 1-800-255-1750, EXT. 2238, OR VISIT US AT OUR WEB SITE AT
HTTP://WWW.WORLDBOOK.COM

GRIMSHAW, CAROLINE.
OUR WORLD / CAROLINE GRIMSHAW; SCIENCE CONSULTANT, JOHN
STRINGER.   P. CM. -- (FOLLOW ME)
"FOLLOW ME AND FIND OUT (ALMOST) EVERYTHING ABOUT YOUR
WORLD!"   INCLUDES INDEX.
SUMMARY: USES BRIEF TEXT, ILLUSTRATIONS, QUIZZES, AND GAMES TO
EXPLAIN ABOUT THE PHYSICAL CHARACTERISTICS OF EARTH, HOW LIFE
BEGAN ON EARTH, AND HOW PEOPLE HAVE INTERACTED WITH THE
PLANET THROUGH HISTORY.
ISBN 0-7166-8800-X (HC). -- ISBN 0-7166-8801-8 (SC).
1. SCIENCE-JUVENILE LITERATURE. 2. EARTH-JUVENILE LITERATURE. 3. LIFE
(BIOLOGY)-JUVENILE LITERATURE. [1. SCIENCE. 2. EARTH. 3. LIFE
(BIOLOGY)] I. TITLE. II. SERIES: FOLLOW ME (CHICAGO, ILL.)
Q163.G75 1997
550--DC21   97-9317
PRINTED IN SPAIN
1 2 3 4 5 6 7 8 9 10 01 00 99 98 97

Welcome to a special book all about Our World

Meet your guides...

Hop

Take a giant hop with this bunny to Show Me panels. These activities will help you see for yourself that the facts you are reading are true. Look out for this hot spot:

 show me

Skip

Skip along to Tricky Test Time panels with this kangaroo. Here you will find puzzles, quizzes, and activities. The answers are on the last page of the book. Watch out for this hot spot:

tricky test time

Jump

Take a looping leap with this flying fish. The Follow Me panels let you choose to move to a page further on in the book. This clever little fish will point out the links between the planet Earth and all the plants and animals that live on it. Follow the fish when you see this hot spot:

 follow me

Look out for all sorts of things hiding on the pages when you see this hot spot:

in hiding

What's inside...

You're just a Hop, Skip, and Jump away from knowing (almost) everything about your world!

Where should you start? Just choose a subject and turn to that page.

Take your pick and let's get going.
follow me

Here's your chance to
Make a plane

What do you need to think about?
Let's take a look at planet Earth.

① What is our planet made of?

The Earth is made up of four main layers. At the center of the Earth lies the inner core – a solid ball made of hot metal.

LOOK AT THIS DIAGRAM

- ☐ INNER CORE
- ☐ OUTER CORE
- ▨ MANTLE
- ▨ CRUST

The crust is the Earth's thin outer layer. The mantle beneath is about 1,800 miles (2,900 kilometers) thick and made of very hot rock. The core is even hotter and is liquid on the outside and solid on the inside.

 show me

A good way to look at the Earth's layers is to make a clay planet. Use four different colors for the layers shown above. First make the ball-shaped inner core, then work outward. Ask an adult to help you cut out a slice.

Around the planet there is a layer of gases called the atmosphere (see below).

 **follow me**

Follow me to page 15 to see how the different gases in the air help keep us alive.

_____ in **hiding** _____

④ Find the nine planets hiding on these pages. Which one is planet Earth?

② How heavy is the Earth?

Our planet weighs about 6,600,000,000,000,000,000,000 short tons (6.0 sextillion metric tons). Every year, it picks up more dust falling from space and gets heavier.

③ How wide is our planet?

The distance around the Earth is about 25,000 miles (40,000 km).

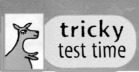

tricky test time

If you walked 2½ miles (4 km) every hour, how many hours would it take you to walk nonstop around the Earth – 2,000, 5,000, or 10,000?

④ What shape is our planet?

The Earth is not a perfect ball. How do we know this? Look at the diagram below.

First the distance around the equator (an imaginary line around the middle of the Earth) is measured. Then the distance around the Earth through the North and South poles is measured. The distance around the equator is 42 miles (67 km) longer, showing us that the Earth is a bit fatter than it is tall.

NORTH POLE

THE EQUATOR

SOUTH POLE

show me

Carefully measure around an orange from top to bottom and then from side to side. Are the measurements the same? Is it a perfect ball?

follow me

How does the weather shape the land? Follow me to page 13.

⑤ Is Earth the only planet?

The Earth is just one of nine planets that spins around a huge star called the sun. The sun and the planets together are called the solar system. There are millions of other solar systems in the universe.

tricky test time

Make your way through this solar system true (**T**) or false (**F**) maze.

START HERE

THE END

Mercury is the closest planet to the sun. **T F**

Jupiter is the smallest planet. **T F**

Saturn's rings are made of gas. **T F**

Uranus was discovered in 1781. **T F**

Venus is the nearest planet to the Earth. **T F**

Mars is known as the "blue planet." **T F**

The Earth is a planet that is always

On the move

Our planet has been changing
for millions of years.

The giant jigsaw

The Earth's crust is not one smooth
piece of rock. It is made up of several
gigantic pieces that float on the
melted rock underneath. These
pieces are called *plates*. They fit
together like a giant jigsaw puzzle.

follow me

What happens when
plates push against
each other? Follow me
to page 8.

LOOK AT THIS MAP

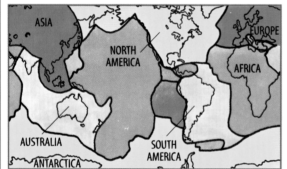

ASIA
EUROPE
NORTH AMERICA
AFRICA
AUSTRALIA
SOUTH AMERICA
ANTARCTICA

This is a flat map of the world. There are about
eight main plates and several smaller ones. They
carry huge land masses called *continents*: Africa,
North America, South America, Antarctica, Asia,
Australia, and Europe.

The Earth's plates move
around very slowly.
So, the continents also
drift around the
planet's surface.
Millions of years ago,
the continents were
all joined together.

CONTINENTS THAT DRIFT

190 MILLION YEARS AGO

120 MILLION YEARS AGO

50 MILLION YEARS AGO

TODAY

The proof

Scientists look at fossils found in rocks. These are the hardened remains of plants and animals that died millions of years ago. Fossils of similar creatures have been found on different continents. Because these creatures could not swim across the oceans, scientists believe that the continents must have once been joined together.

LYSTROSAURUS
Fossils of this plant-eating reptile have been found in Asia, South Africa, and Antarctica.

in hiding
Find four fossils hiding on these pages.

follow me
To see how plants and animals are adapted to survive in their surroundings, follow me to page 16.

show me
Find an atlas. On paper, trace around the shapes of the continents. Then, cut around the shapes and try to fit them together.

Climates change too.

Hot places, such as deserts, may have been freezing cold in the past. Places that are cold today may have once been very hot. As the continents drift, they move from hot areas to cold areas, or the other way around. This happens very slowly, over millions of years.

tricky test time

Follow the lines to find out how the weather in each place has changed.

450 million years ago: empty wasteland totally covered with ice.

50 million years ago: very hot, with crocodile-infested swamps.

18,000 years ago: a layer of ice 820 feet (250 meters) thick covered the top half of this continent.

1,000 years ago: this island was warm enough to raise sheep.

GREENLAND

NORTH AMERICA

ENGLAND

SAHARA

show me
Find a tree stump and look at it. Every year, a tree grows a new ring around its trunk. Trees grow more in warmer weather. As a result, the rings are wider in warmer years. Count the rings to work out how old the tree is. Then, look to see which year was the warmest.

WHO CAME UP WITH THIS IDEA?
A German scientist named Alfred Wegener wrote about moving continents in 1912. He called this movement continental drift. He showed that ice once covered places that are hot today, such as Africa and Brazil.

Let's examine the

Look of the land

Have you ever wondered why the land is shaped as it is?

Moving plates

The shifting plates of the Earth's crust either move away from each other, scrape against each other, or move toward each other. Where these plates meet, the land buckles, bends, or is pulled apart, making earthquakes, volcanoes, mountains, and geysers.

① Earthquakes

These happen along the edges of the plates. Two plates suddenly slip and make shock waves, which cause the ground to move.

This photograph was taken after an earthquake in Japan. Many homes, railroads, and roads were destroyed.

tricky test time

The strength of an earthquake affects objects and land in different ways. Can you put these five pictures in order, starting with the effects of the least violent earthquake and ending with the most violent?

A. B. C. D. E.

② Volcanoes

Melted rock, called *lava*, forces its way up from the mantle through cracks in the Earth's crust, making volcanoes. The shape of the volcano depends on the kind of rock and how violently it erupts.

This photograph was taken as the Kilauea volcano on the island of Hawaii erupted.

tricky test time

Follow the lines and match the types of volcanoes with their pictures.

CINDER CONE
Volcano has steep slopes.

SHIELD
Volcano has gentle slopes.

STRATA
Volcano is cone-shaped.

in hiding

There are 2 shield and 3 strata volcanoes hiding on these pages. Find them!

This photograph shows the Rocky Mountains in North America. They are 70 million years old.

③ Mountains

When two plates smash into each other, the land crumples. If this land folds upward, huge fold mountains may be made.

show me

Make your own mountain by sliding two flat pieces of clay together until they fold upward.

follow me

Follow me to page 13 to see how the look of the land is changed by the weather.

④ Geysers

Geysers are very hot jets of steam and water that shoot out of the ground more than 100 feet (30 m).

About every hour Old Faithful in Yellowstone National Park spouts around 10,000 gallons (38,000 liters) of water into the air.

follow me

Follow me to page 10 and find out about boiling jets of water under the ocean floor.

The wonderful world of
Water

Nearly three-quarters of our planet is covered by water. Let's take a look at it.

in hiding

Find the six sea creatures hidden on these pages.

96.5% of all water is SALTY.

Nearly all the Earth's water is salty. It is found in the seas and oceans. This is a photo of the largest ocean, the Pacific Ocean, which covers almost one-third of the planet.

The water is salty mainly because rivers flowing into the ocean pass over rocks that contain salt. Most of the salt is lost from seawater when it freezes, for example, when icebergs form.

show me

Make an ice cube from clean, salty water. When you lick the ice cube, you will find that much of the salt has disappeared.

1 HOW HOT IS THE SEA?

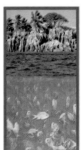

The top of an ocean can be as hot as 79 °F (26 °C), while the bottom may be close to freezing. This is because the sun's heat does not pass through water very easily. But in some places, very hot water, about 750 °F (400 °C), gushes from cracks in the ocean floor.

2 HOW DEEP IS THE SEA?

The deepest place on Earth is the Mariana Trench in the Pacific Ocean. It is 36,198 feet (11,033 m) deep, which is 7,170 feet (2,193 m) deeper than Mount Everest is tall!

3.5% of all water is FRESH.

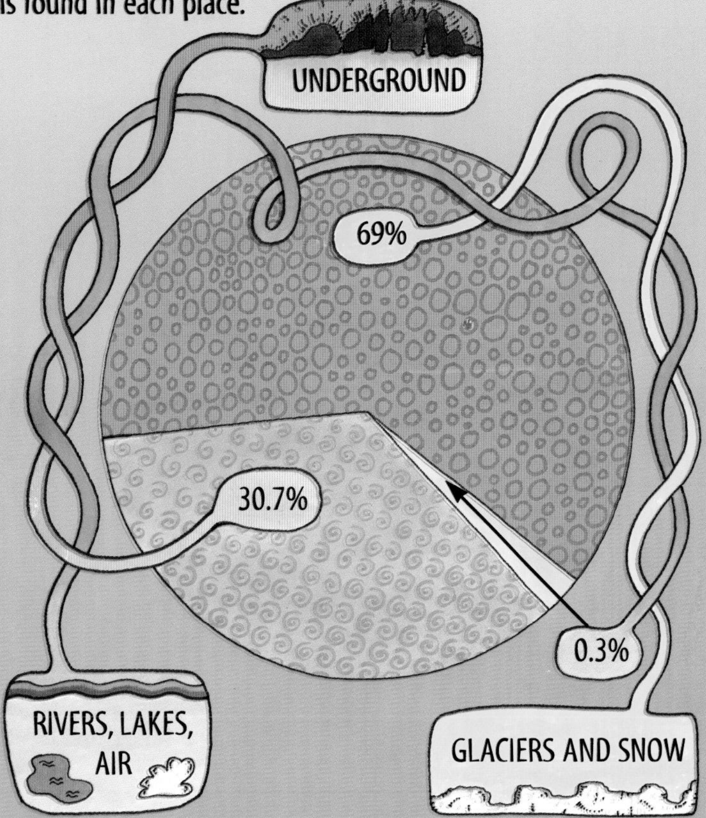

follow me

Why do we need water to survive? Follow me to page 15.

tricky test time

Fresh water is found underground and in rivers, lakes, glaciers, snow, and the air. Look at this chart. Then, follow the maze lines to find out how much of the total amount of fresh water is found in each place.

UNDERGROUND

69%

30.7%

0.3%

RIVERS, LAKES, AIR

GLACIERS AND SNOW

A glacier is a large river of ice that moves very slowly down a mountain.

show me

Fill a bowl with water, then blow across the surface of it. The harder you blow, the larger the waves are.

follow me

Follow me to page 13 to see what happens if a place doesn't have enough water.

3 WATER THAT MOVES

Each day, the oceans move back and forth as tides. Tides are caused by the pull of the moon as it circles the Earth. When the sea moves up onto the land, we call it high tide. When it moves out again, we call it low tide.

Wind blowing across the sea causes waves to form on the surface of the water.

Our planet can be
Hot or cold, wet

Why do different places have different amounts of sunshine, rain, and wind, and how does this shape the land?

WEATHER
The weather is the amount of sunshine, rain, and wind at any particular time.

CLIMATE
The climate is the most typical weather of a particular place.

What makes a place hot or cold?

1 WHERE YOU ARE ON THE EARTH

The closer you are to the equator, the hotter it is. This is because the sun shines directly on the equator but shines at an angle on the poles.

NORTH POLE
THE EQUATOR
EARTH
SOUTH POLE

Hot at the equator.

Cold at the icy North Pole.

2 WHAT SEASON YOU ARE IN

The Earth takes one year to move around the sun. The Earth is slightly tilted. So, during the year, parts of the Earth are closer to the sun. This causes the seasons. The parts that are tilted toward the sun receive more sunlight and heat.

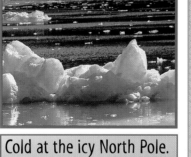

AUTUMN
SPRING
WINTER
SUMMER
SUMMER
WINTER
SPRING
AUTUMN

follow me

Follow me to page 15 to see how the sun keeps plants and animals alive.

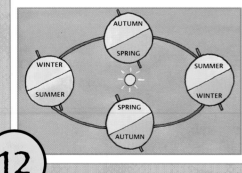

dry...

in hiding

Find six snowflakes hidden on these pages. Two of the snowflakes are the same. Which two?

Can the weather be dangerous?

THE WEATHER CAN BE TOO DRY

When there is not enough rain, a country may have a water shortage called a *drought*. The ground becomes dry and it may crack. It becomes too dry for plants to grow and there is not enough water for people to drink.

THE WEATHER CAN BE TOO WET

Heavy rain may cause rivers to overflow, flooding the land. Hurricanes, or typhoons, are violent storms with wind and rain that travel up to twice as fast as a speeding train!

show me

Leave a piece of clay to dry in the sun. What happens to the clay when it dries out?

How does the weather shape the land?

The Earth's surface is being worn away all the time. How does this happen?

IN COLD WEATHER

Rain water freezes in the cracks of the Earth, forcing them wider apart. When the water melts, bits of the rock fall off.

show me

See how water expands by filling a straw with water and closing both ends with clay. Put the straw in the freezer for a few hours. The water freezes and forces the clay out of the straw.

WIND POWER

Wind may blow stone or sand against rocks, breaking them down. Rivers and glaciers also carry bits of stone that rub against surrounding rocks.

CHEMICAL ACTION

Chemicals in the rain may wear away rocks and cause them to change shape. Spectacular stalactites and stalagmites may form where water drips through rocks.

tricky test time

These strange landforms were made by wind and water wearing away the rock. Match the pictures to their names.

A   B   C

WAVE ROCK (AUSTRALIA)   ROCK PILLARS (ISRAEL)   HOODOOS (CANADA)

Life on Earth

Why is there life on Earth and how does the planet support it?

Nearly everything that is alive is made of cells. This is a cell. •••••➤

LOOKING FOR LIFE ON OTHER PLANETS

Spacecrafts have photographed other planets, but scientists have not yet discovered life on any of them. In 1996, however, scientists claimed that they had evidence of life on Mars from millions of years ago. They believed that the rock they had found from Mars contained fossils of tiny creatures made of only one cell.

ONE CELL

An ameba is a tiny creature made of only one cell.

MILLIONS OF CELLS

People are made up of more than 10 trillion (10,000,000,000,000 cells).

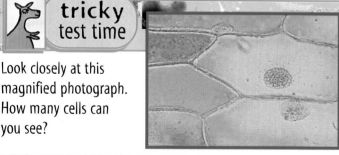

tricky test time

Look closely at this magnified photograph. How many cells can you see?

It was too hot for anything to live on Earth when it formed 4,600 million years ago. Slowly, the planet cooled down. But it was not until 1,000 million years later that the first living creatures started to appear in the Earth's water.

follow me

To see how life on Earth has been changing through the years, follow me to page 16.

The planet lets us live. How?

① It gives us air to breathe.

We need air to survive. The air is made up of different gases, but oxygen is the gas we need to breathe to keep us alive.

People breathe in oxygen. This helps give us energy. ······▶ People breathe out carbon dioxide.

Plants give out oxygen. ◀····· Plants take in carbon dioxide and oxygen. This helps them grow.

follow me

When does the air become dangerous to breathe? Follow me to page 22.

in hiding

There are four amebas hiding on these pages. Can you find them?

② It gives us water to drink.

All plants and animals are made up of water. Almost two-thirds of a person's body is made up of water because your insides need to be kept wet all the time.

Water carries all the chemicals we need around our bodies. Water also helps keep our bodies cool.

We lose water every day through breathing, sweating, and urinating. We need to drink regularly to replace this water.

show me

Seeds can grow in the dark, but plants need sunlight to grow. Ask an adult to plant some seeds in a pot. Leave them on a window sill. Watch how the growing shoots turn to face the sun during the day.

③ It feeds us.

All living things depend on the light and warmth of the sun. Plants use sunlight, a gas called carbon dioxide, and water from the air to make food. Animals eat plants, or other animals, and these animals are then eaten by other animals. This is called a food chain.

tricky test time

The links in this food chain are muddled. Can you put them in the right order?

A Caterpillars are eaten by sparrows.

B Leaves of the tree are eaten by caterpillars.

C Sparrows are eaten by hawks.

D Sunshine gives trees energy to grow.

It's all a question of Survival

We know that the Earth's climates and landscapes are always changing. Plants and animals also change over millions of years, so that they are able to cope with their new surroundings. This is called adaptation.

follow me

To see how people adapt to where they live, follow me to page 20.

tricky test time

These plants and animals have all adapted to the places where they live. Match the names, labels, and pictures.

POLAR BEAR

A This animal has large, strong front feet for digging.

1

VENUS'S FLYTRAP

B This plant has spines, which help protect it.

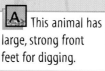
2

MOLE

C This animal has thick fur and lives in cold climates.

3

CACTUS

D This plant grows in poor soil, so it also eats insects!

4

Looking at lif

YEAR: 570 million years ago

Animals with shells, such as trilobites, live in the water. There are no plants or animals living on the land. Are there still animals with shells on Earth today?

YEAR: 435 million years ago

The first fish swim in the water. The first land plants, such as mosses, start to grow.

YEAR: 360 mill years ag

There are forests on Earth. Anim invade the land. These animals, call amphibians, can live both the water ar on the land.

Look at these photographs. See how living things have special features to help them survive in their surroundings. Deserts are very dry places, so it can be difficult for animals to find food. A camel carries its own food supply in a hump on its back. Desert plants do not grow near each other. By being spread out, they can get water from a wide area.

ice the beginning of time

YEAR:	YEAR:	YEAR:	YEAR:
330 million years ago	248 million years ago	65 million years ago	2 million years ago

e first reptiles e on land. Their aly skin stops em from losing ater. Can you ink of animals th scales that ll live on the rth today?

The first dinosaurs walk the planet. Some early reptiles fly in the sky, where there is less chance of being killed.

The dinosaurs become extinct and mammals — such as cows, horses, pigs, and elephants — roam the Earth.

The first humans appear on the planet. They have heavy bones, thick skins, and furry bodies to protect them from the cold.

follow me

Follow me to page 18 to find out how humans have explored the planet.

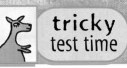
tricky test time

Imagine that all the time since the birth of the Earth was squeezed into one year. If the Earth was born on January 1, can you guess how long after that date it was that the first humans appeared? Was it July 4, September 15, or December 31?

in hiding

There are five animals hiding on these pages. Which one do you think arrived on Earth first?

Learning to Understand

People have always been curious to know more about their planet. They explore it and make maps of what they find.

Explorers

Why have people explored the planet?

◇ To look for treasure, such as gold.

◇ To look for a new home in a new land.

◇ To look for new ways to make money.

◇ To look for fun and adventure.

If you were going to explore the planet, what would you look for?

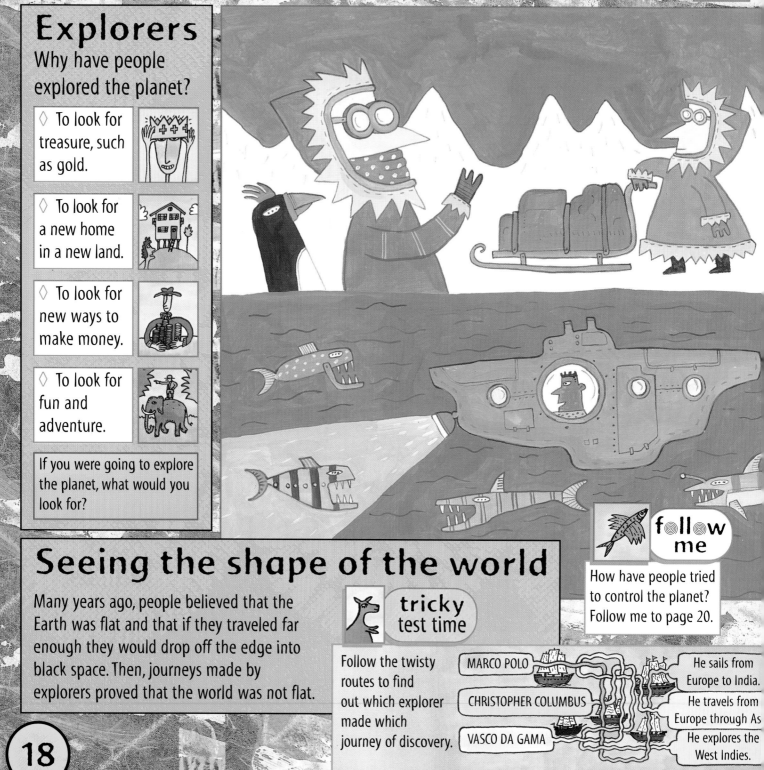

follow me

How have people tried to control the planet? Follow me to page 20.

Seeing the shape of the world

Many years ago, people believed that the Earth was flat and that if they traveled far enough they would drop off the edge into black space. Then, journeys made by explorers proved that the world was not flat.

tricky test time

Follow the twisty routes to find out which explorer made which journey of discovery.

MARCO POLO

CHRISTOPHER COLUMBUS

VASCO DA GAMA

He sails from Europe to India.

He travels from Europe through As

He explores the West Indies.

THE FREEZING SOUTH POLE

In 1911, a Norwegian, Roald Amundsen, became the first man to reach the South Pole. In a long race across the ice, he beat the Englishman Robert Scott by five weeks.

DIVING REALLY DEEP

Until recently, scientists did not know what the dark ocean floors looked like. Now, they have special machines that they send down to explore deep waters.

follow me

o find out how we re destroying the lanet, follow me to age 22.

Pictures of the planet

Maps help us understand our planet. People draw maps in many different ways, depending on the information they want to show.

in hiding

A compass helps you find your way around. It has an arrow that always points north. Can you spot the three compasses hidden on these pages?

 show me

Look carefully at these maps. On one, you can see the land features of the area, such as rivers, forests, and mountains. Some maps show where roads and railroads are. Others pinpoint the position of buildings.

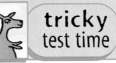 **tricky test time**

Maps use special pictures, or symbols, to stand for different things. A key tells you what the symbols represent. Most maps are divided up into squares. To find a square, use the numbers on the side of the map and the letters at the top. One square is labeled to help you. Now use the key and the map to answer the questions. What is found in these squares: 4A, 2B, 3D? Which square has a palm tree in it?

THIS IS SQUARE 2C.

KEY

PALM TREE   RIVER   ROAD   MOUNTAIN

People and the planet—
Control it! Use

People need to protect themselves from the climate so that they can survive. They also try to use the planet's natural resources, such as water, oil, and gas.

How we survive

1

THE HEAT
We use electric fans and air conditioning. We paint our walls white to reflect the sun's heat. These things keep the inside of the house cooler.

2

THE COLD
We burn fuel and build our houses with thick, solid walls to keep out the cold.

3

THE WET
We build houses on stilts to protect them from floods. We have drainage systems so that the water flows away from the streets.

4

THE DRY
We take water from lakes and rivers, and direct it to dry areas. This is called *irrigation*.

show me

On a hot day, see if you can feel the difference between wearing dark clothes and white clothes. White clothes keep you cooler because they reflect the sun's heat. Dark clothes absorb the heat.

tricky test time

People from different parts of the world behave in different ways in hot climates. Work out the problems to find out how hot it is in the places shown.

BOMBAY, INDIA
15 + 12 + 13 + 19 + 26 = ? °F
5 + 2 + 3 + 9 + 11 = ? °C

MIAMI, FLORIDA
30 − 8 + 14 + 30 + 19 = ? °F
20 − 8 + 4 + 10 + 4 = ? °C

Using our planet

FARMING THE LAND

About 10,000 years ago, people started farming – growing plants and keeping animals on their land. Today, some small farms grow just enough to feed their own families. Larger farms may sell some of their food to other people.

follow me

How are we poisoning the soil? Follow me to page 23.

USING THE EARTH'S POWER

1 WATER POWER

People control water by building dams. These structures are barriers that hold back water and stop land from flooding. Water is stored next to dams in large lakes called *reservoirs*. The stored water flows through machines called turbines, producing electric power.

2 OIL AND GAS

People dig deep into the Earth to find oil and gas. Oil is used to power cars and airplanes. We use gas in our homes for cooking and heating.

show me

Make a dam. Ask an adult to cut off the top of a plastic bottle and then make holes along the side of the bottle. Cover the holes with your fingers and then, over a sink, ask a friend to pour water into the bottle. When it is full, take your fingers away and watch the water shoot out. Your fingers are like a dam, holding back the water.

in hiding

nd the six farm nimals hidden on ese pages.

People and the planet—

Destroy it.

The temperature and atmosphere of our planet are perfect for supporting life. But people are starting to damage the planet. If this continues, they may upset the conditions that let us survive.

We are polluting the air we breathe.

Cars and factories pollute the Earth by pouring smoke and poisonous gases into the air. Burning waste and forests can also cause dangerous gases to pollute the air. This pollution may affect people, causing dizziness, headaches, and even cancer.

show me

The next time you go for a walk along a busy street, look around you. Can you see any dirty smoke coming out of cars or buildings? What does the air smell like?

We are harming trees and buildings.

The gases that pollute our air sometimes dissolve in the raindrops in the air. This makes acid rain, which destroys trees and harms buildings.

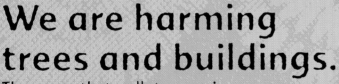

WE ARE UPSETTING THE EARTH'S TEMPERATURE

The smoke and gases are not only making the air dirty, they are also making the world warmer. Instead of disappearing into space, the gases float above the Earth. The heat that rises from the Earth cannot escape through this layer of gases. As a result, the air stays warm. This is called the *greenhouse effect*.

show me

The gases let more heat in than they let out – just like a greenhouse. Walk into a greenhouse on a sunny day. Is it warmer inside or outside the greenhouse?

Save it!

in hiding

Hidden on these pages are three things we use every day that pollute the planet: a car, a plastic bag, and a can. Find them!

WE ARE LEAVING OURSELVES UNPROTECTED

There is a layer of a special type of gas called *ozone* high in the atmosphere. It stops the sun's harmful rays from reaching the Earth. But pollution is destroying this protection. The dark blue area in this photograph shows the hole in the ozone layer.

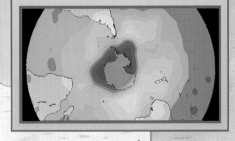

Let's all stop and think.

It's not too late to save the planet. What can we do? Think about…

1 OUR GARBAGE

The things we throw away do not always break down. They may put poisons into the soil. We are also running out of land for burying our used paper, bottles, cans, plastics, and other garbage. We need to recycle as much as possible.

2 OUR TRANSPORT

Cars pollute the air. Try to walk, ride a bicycle, or use public transportation rather than use a car.

3 MAKE AN EFFORT

Remember, every time you turn off a light, or use a plastic bag more than once, you are helping save the planet. Your effort can make a difference.

tricky test time

Not all power pollutes our planet. Match the pictures to the type of clean, natural power being produced.

A	B	C
WIND POWER	SOLAR POWER	WATER POWER

Wars destroy the planet.

In the Persian Gulf War in 1991, ships carrying oil were attacked. Eight million barrels of oil spilled into the sea, polluting the water and killing birds and fish.

So that's the end of your journey. Now you know (almost) everything about your world!

tricky test time

THE ANSWERS P5: (top) 10,000 hours; (bottom). F – Jupiter is the biggest planet, Pluto is the smallest planet; T; T; F – Mars is known as the "red planet"; F – Saturn's rings are made of pieces of icy rock; T. P7: 450 MYA = Sahara; 50 MYA = England; 18,000 YA = North America; 1,000 YA = Greenland. P8: C, A, E, B, D. P9: left = strata; center = cinder cone; right = shield. P11: glaciers and snow = 69%; underground = 30.7%; rivers, lakes, air = 0.3%. P13: A = Hoodoos; B = Wave Rock; C = rock pillars. P14: seven cells. P15: D, B, A, C. p16: polar bear = C4; Venus's flytrap = D1; mole = A2; cactus = B3. P17: December 31. P18: Marco Polo = Europe – India; Christopher Columbus = West Indies; Vasco da Gama = Europe – Asia. P19: 4A = mountain; 2B = river; 3D = road; the palm tree is in square 1C. P20: the people in the pictures are coping with the heat in different ways, even though it is actually 85 °F (30 °C) in both pictures. P23: A = water power; B = wind power; C = solar power.

PICTURE CREDITS Cover: Top left: Science Photo Library; bottom left: Ace; top right Zefa; bottom right; Robert Harding. Back cover : Top: Britstock; right: Science Photo Library; bottom: Pictor. Inside: P1 Science Photo Library. P3 Top left, top right, center top right, center right, bottom left: Science Photo Library; center left: Robert Harding; bottom right: Planet Earth Pictures. P4 Top, bottom: Science Photo Library. P5 Left, right: Science Photo Library. P7 Top left: Planet Earth Pictures; bottom left: AKG; right: Pictor. P8 Popperfoto. P9 Top right, bottom right: Pictor; top left: Science Photo Library P10 Left: Science Photo Library; right: Britstock. P11 Top: Science Photo Library; bottom: Zefa. P12 Left: Tony Stone; right: Pictor. P13 Top left, top right: Robert Harding; top center, bottom left: Science Photo Library; bottom center: Pictor; bottom right: Zefa. P14 Center left, bottom: Science Photo Library; top, center right: Tony Stone. P15 Top: Tony Stone; center: Pictor; bottom: Science Photo Library. P16 Top: Pictor; top center, bottom center: Tony Stone; bottom: Science Photo Library. P17 Left: Pictor; right: Tony Stone. P19 Right: maps © Crown 85069M/ Ordnance Survey; © RV Reise-und Verkehrsverlag © Kartographie; Geo Data; Swiss Nat. Map 1:25,000 ©Swiss Fed. Office. Top left: Hulton Getty; bottom left: Oxford Scientific Films. P20 Top left, top left center, bottom left center, far right, right: Tony Stone; bottom: Science Photo Library. P21 Top right, center right: Tony Stone; bottom: Science Photo Library. P22 Top: Tony Stone; bottom: Science Photo Library. P23 Top right, top left, bottom left, bottom center right: Science Photo Library; bottom center left: Tony Stone; right: Pictor.